Change UR Mind,
Change UR Life:
A Pocketbook of Quotes

Introduction

O pen your eyes. Don't just open your eyes. Look at your surroundings. What is happening behind your back? Beneath the self-conscious? In the reality of your mind? How did those thoughts get there? How do they make you feel? What could have been shown, told, or seen that could have changed your perception of self, others, or life in general?

"Your mind is able to manifest things into reality."

–UNKNOWN

We are the alpha race of all animals, yet we behave as though we are separated by a minor difference or two.

I grew up in the Greater Toronto Area (GTA) in Canada, more specifically Durham Region (Pickering, Ajax, Whitby, etc.). Here I was trained to mask my true self and become who I needed to be depending on the situation. We all have our roles to play in life. This is why I always say,

"Life is a game, and I live in Canada with monopoly money!"

It was confusing as a child going to a Catholic school during the day, and a Pentecostal/Christian/Anglican/Tabernacle to praise at night. I was in the church choir, went to the youth group Friday night meetings and church every Sunday. I can vividly recall in grade 8 when responding to a question in regards to my Holy Sacrament of Confirmation ritual, I started to say, "The pastor was telling us that…", when my teacher quickly interrupted me and said, "You mean the Priest?" I was taken aback and just said, "Yea that's what I mean."

The fundamental ideas were always the same. Heaven is good like GOD, and Hell is evil like the devil. When I got to high school, I had to take a compulsory course in 'World Religions'. It changed my life. I was exposed to multiple ways to show gratitude to the Creator.

At 16 years old, it dawned on me that we ARE the world, we ARE all different, so ARE our languages, why not our religions? I then became uncomfortable with literal interpretations of The Holy Bible, with all its ritualistic ceremonies, and became obsessed with learning about the Illuminati, secret societies, and other conspiracy theories.

"By changing what goes into our minds we can change so much of what comes out of them."

–KERRY BLACKBURN

Watching television all day, every day; being programmed to believe everything I saw, lead me to believe that my life could be like 'Sex In The City' or '90210'. Yet, nothing I did ever compared to the happiness I saw in the eyes of the great actors. I expected my life to play out as it does on television. Boy was I disappointed when my prom didn't look like a wedding and my Mr. Big didn't have a driver's license, much less a car. I expected that my life would be perfect with no flaws, and I wanted what I saw others have. I decided to become an actor, a storyteller, and a teacher because I love to share, and wanted to use my gifts to have a positive impact on the world.

"Trade all your expectations for appreciation and your whole world changes in an instant."

-TONY ROBBINS

Once I realized the truth in, "Please and thank you are the magic words", I began my journey; which I will continuously be on until I pass, into a life of GRATITUDE.

"An attitude of gratitude is one of the most powerful instruments of change in the world."

-UNKNOWN

I began to see all of my accomplishments as just that ACCOMPLISHMENTS. No longer can I look at the negative and dwell there. In 2003 I was officially diagnosed with Bipolar Type 2 disorder, and another aspect of my journey began. Bipolar 2 is similar to Bipolar 1, with moods cycling between high and low without reaching full-blown mania.

MANIA:

Mental Illness is marked by periods of great excitement, euphoria, delusions, and overactivity.

I was now labeled as being a MENTAL HEALTH PATIENT.

"Labels HELP define you, but THEY ARE NOT YOU!"

-Colin Wright

There are trials and tribulations every day associated with a bipolar diagnosis. The highs are awesomely awesome, I feel like I am at the top of the world, where my ideas and my life are validated. The lows are depressing; anything and everything can affect, effect, and cause me to want to end my life. I have been on and off medication for years. Some medications work well, some cause me to be dependent on them, some cause weight gain, some assist with sleep, and some make me feel average, normal, like a drone. I am aware of the benefits of medication and how it can help. Yet my main medication must begin with the food that I eat and the energy in which I surround myself.

"Let food be thy medicine, and medicine thy food"

-Hippocrates

In 2012 I decided to make some active changes in the way I think. The thoughts that I allow into my mind come from within, and only I can make the necessary adjustments. One thing I chose to do was write quotes in my special book. When I was hospitalized in Brampton Ontario for 28 days my father bought me a little red journal to collect my racing thoughts. The journal was titled " Keep Calm and Move on". On the walls of the mental health unit, there were pictures from other patients, and some of them had quotes on them. After reading the following quote I felt inspired to not give up and fulfill my purpose.

"Life is one big road with a lot of signs. So when you riding through the ruts, don't complicate your mind. Flee from hate, mischief and jealousy. Don't bury your thoughts, put your vision to reality. Wake Up and Live!"

-BOB MARLEY

I had to keep this quote with me and wrote it in the back of my journal. That same day I was reading a book when another quote caught my attention and I had to write it down as well. It didn't matter where I went I had my red book with me, and it didn't matter who you were if you said something that had substance I would ask you to repeat and tell you one day I will write a book and quote you. When I feel depressed, overwhelmed, manic, or worthless I can pull out my book of quotes and just read. Usually, by the time I read three or four, and reflect on where I am in the present moment I am in a better mood. What I have done is collected my favorite quotes and categorized them for you. The quotes may not have the original phrasing or author, yet the people whom I have quoted are my reference, and quotes are written to my inner-standing.

As you read Cooki's Scribes To Positive Thinking, I ask that you take it with you on your daily journey, meditate on the quotes, and use my personal stories for reference. Also, this book is not meant to be read in sequential order. As you move throughout your day and something disrupts your vibe; pull out this book and choose a chapter that relates to what you are dealing with. Then open any page on that chapter and read 3-6 quotes, and I know you will have a new inner-standing. I am grateful for this opportunity to share my collection of quotes with you.

Namaste,
Christie Maingot
@Cookimango_da_goddess

Table of Contents

Life

As a Caribbean Canadian child, it became clear to me at a young age that I was different. I was a very obedient and compassionate child who was always willing to help and be accepted. My parents argued a lot, daily, and it recently dawned on me that my hesitation to defend myself stems from this childhood experience. I had lived my life to please others and deprived myself of what true happiness is. Once we leave the comfort of our mother's womb, we are alone on this earth. The process of learning and discovering who we are, and what our purpose is can be difficult if we are not PHYSICALLY, MENTALLY, and, SPIRITUALLY ready.

"The summit of happiness is reached when a person is ready to be what he is."
—DESIDERIUS ERASMUS

"It's NOT what we do but HOW we do that determines satisfaction."
—UNKNOWN

The word vocation comes from the Latin word vocare meaning "to call". The idea that work is a calling...

"Live the questions."
—RAINER MARIA RILKE

"Hope is the cordial that keeps life from
stagnation."
—SAM RICHARDSON

"Real generosity towards the future lies in giving all to the present."
—ALBERT CAMS

"Muddy Water... Let stand... Becomes...
CLEAR."
—TAO TE CHING

"In matters of style, swim with the current; in
the matters of principle, stand like a rock."
—THOMAS JEFFERSON

4 CARDINAL VIRTUES: Prudence,
Justice, Temperance & Fortitude
--PLATO

1.Prudence [prood-ns]
noun
good judgment or wisdom gained from
experience
2. Justice [juhs-tis]
noun
the quality of fairness, and treating everyone
the same
3. Temperance [tem-pruh ns]
noun
moderation and self-restraint
4. Fortitude [fawr-ti-tyood]
noun
mental and emotional strength that allows a
person to endure pain or adversity with courage

"Truth involves seeing things as they are."
—UNKNOWN

"Values are immaterial if we don't embody them. They are the moral backbone that lets us stand up to the challenges in life."
—UNKNOWN

"This very moment is always the only moment."
—MARTHA BECK

"There is no way you can be successful in life if your children are not successful."
—TED TURNER

Tao gives all things life,
Te gives them fulfillment,
Nature is what shapes them,
Living is what brings them to completion.
—TAO TE CHING

"Reality is nothing but a collective hunch.
Individual interpretations will differ. Two people
experiencing the same event will recall different
elements of it."
—LILLY TOMLIN

"Happiness is a feeling NOT an accumulation of
experiences."
—ANDREA F. POLARD

"Our life is frittered away by detail. Simplify,
simplify."
—HENERY DAVID THOREAU

"If possible, so far as it depends on you, be at peace with all men."
—ROMANS 12:8

"Nothing that comes my way will sour my day."
—JOEL OSTEEN

"Don't let one family member who won't show you respect let you get off course."
—JOEL OSTEEN

"Do not boast about tomorrow for you do not know what the day may bring."
—PROVERBS 27:1

"We are where we are because that's exactly
where we wanna be."
—ICE

"You need to know who you are to become who
you are supposed to be."
—COOKI MANGO

" In order to look out you gotta look within."
-JAHTE

"Wake up every morning fixed on determination
so we can go to be with satisfaction."
—KERRY BLACKBURN

"Life has no limitations except the
ones you make."
–LES BROWN

"Breathe, let go, and remind yourself that this
very moment is the only one you know
you have for sure."
–OPRAH

"If you love life then don't waste time for
time is what life is made up of."
–BRUCE LEE

"Every day is an opportunity to do
something better."
–UNKNOWN

"Life is a function of your desires multiplied by your expectations divided by your choices."
—IYANLA VANZANT

"We are not robots, we have emotion."
—MILLIE BUCKS

"Everyday is a present. Open it with excitement, celebration, and gratitude."
—KERRY BLACKBURN

"To accomplish great things, we must NOT only act but also dream; not only plan, but believe."
—KERRY BLACKBURN

"We may not have it all together but together
we have it all."
—JD KEYS

"Your life doesn't just happen. Whether you
know it or not, it is carefully designed by you."
—STEPHEN COVEY

"Nobody really knows why they are alive until
they know what they would die for."
—MARTIN LUTHER KING

"Everyday in every way, I am is going to get
better and better."
—EMILE COUE

"Live like you have limited time."
—JOEL OSTEEN

"YOLO: You Only Live Once."
—DRAKE

"Judge each day not by the harvest you reap
but by the seeds you plant."
—JOEL OSTEEN

"If you want a quality life… Ask quality
questions."
—UNKNOWN

"Happiness is not something you get in life. It is
something that you bring to life."
—DR. WAYNE W. DYER

"Life is like a camera; focus on what's
important, capture the good times, develop
from the negatives, and if it goes wrong…
Take another shot."
—UNKNOWN

Disappointments are just God's way of saying,
'I've got something better. Be patient, live life,
and have faith.'"
—LANETTE SEM

"Life is one big road with a lot of signs.
So when you riding through the ruts, don't
complicate your mind. Flee from hate, mischief
and jealousy. Don't bury your thoughts, put your
vision to reality. Wake Up and Live!"
—BOB MARLEY

"Children have cents they require adult help to
make billion$."
—COOKI MANGO

Change

As a Canadian, we have four seasons and should be well-adjusted to the weather changes. Trees are such a great visualization of change; they bloom flowers, create leaves, and shelter. When the climate or circumstance changes, they let go of their leaves knowing that it is not benefiting them anymore. I had always been uncomfortable with change as a child and needed reassurance from outside of myself. Once we as spiritual beings can accept that change needs to occur for us to grow, we will then be able to become our full selves.

"Come out of the circle of time, and into the circle of love."
—RUMI

"Even if we can't change the reality of a situation we can choose our response."
—UNKNOWN

"No great thing is created suddenly. There MUST be TIME. Give your best and always be kind."
—EPICTETUS

"The bigger the dream the smaller the first step."
—DONNA BRAZILE

"When you feel sorry for yourself the best thing you can do is help someone else. Success finally came to me when I stopped worrying so much about finding it."
—PATRICIA HEATON

"Our memories change as we change and begin to see facets of the past in a different light."
—UNKNOWN

"One determined person can make a significant difference, and a group of determined people can change the course of history."
—KERRY BLACKBURN

"If you don't understand your value you will never tap into it."
—UNKNOWN

"Accept yourself when in the process of changing. Guilt will cause you to do worse."
—UNKNOWN

"Be ready for what you are asking for."
—UNKNOWN

"We control what we put out there but we don't control when and how opportunities will come."
—KERRY BLACKBURN

"As long as you have life you have chance."
—LES BROWN

"The longer I live the more I realize the impact of attitude on life. Attitude to me is more important than facts, past, education, money, circumstances, failures, successes, perception, etc. The remarkable thing is we have a choice everyday regarding the attitude we will embrace for that day."
—UNKNOWN

"We can't change the way people act the only thing we can do is play on the one string we have, and that is our ATTITUDE."
—UNKNOWN

"Impossible is just a big word thrown around by small people who find it easier to live in the world they have been given than to explore the power they have to change it."
—KERRY BLACKBURN

"The choices are yours right? You choose happiness, you choose sadness, you choose success, you choose failure, you choose encouragement, and you choose fear. Every moment and opportunity gives you a choice and a chance to do things differently; to produce more positive results."
—STEPHEN COVEY

"What would motivate you to risk everything? What is your cause? Do not be afraid to stand for what you believe in even if it means standing alone."
—KERRY BLACKBURN

"The woman who follows the crowd will usually get no further than the crowd. The woman who walks alone is likely to find herself in places no one has ever been."
—ALBERT EINSTEIN

"Act like you are supposed to be there and you will fit in."
—UNKNOWN

"The level of energy given to your dreams is directly proportional to the speed in which your dreams become your reality."
—UNKNOWN

"If you don't take a chance you don't stand a chance. Plan on taking chances if you want to get anywhere in life. God gives every bird his worm but He does not throw it into the nest."
—UNKNOWN

"The only thing constant in life is change."
—FRANCOIS DE LA ROCHEFOUCAULD

Fear

False Evidence Appears Real.......... Personally fear has caused me to miss out on some great moments in life. I have had a fear of rejection, disappointment, of not being good enough. The negative self-talk can become quite addictive. It has been said that it is easier for the brain to process a negative emotion than it is a positive one. Here are some quotes that have helped me to see past the fog of fear.

"There is no formula for finding happiness or love that lasts. Each person, each couple must come at their own calculus."
—UNKNOWN

"Set aside old hurts and allow yourself to be fully present."
—UNKNOWN

"Laugh at the opposition."
—DONNA BRAZILE

"Longing does not lead to happiness."
—UNKNOWN

"Quit listening to the accusing voices."
—JOEL OSTEEN

"Exchange your fear for faith. You never know who needs to hear what you have to say."
—ROMANS 8:15

"Sometimes we bring an umbrella outside preparing yourself for rain when really it's been sunny all along. Think positive and you will get it in return."
—DANIEL GIBSON

"When hanging onto the wrong thing, the right thing can't get in."
—UNKNOWN

"Accept the fact that disappointment will come."
—VOICE OF HOPE

"We make pressure; pressure don't make us."
—KERRY BLACKBURN

"Our greatest weakness lies in giving up."
—THOMAS EDISON

"Just once do what others say you can't do and
you will never pay attention to their limitation again.
Breaking free of limitations can become a habit
just like living in limitation. Once you get the feeling
that arises from doing what others say cannot be
done. Your mind actually becomes wired to break
those barriers others put in front of you. Success
then becomes a matter of how far you can see you
separating from these limits."
—JAMES COOK

"It's not the challenges we face that strengthen us, rather the process of overcoming them that make us a better person."
—KERRY BLACKBURN

"...don't let your left hand know what your right hand does."
—MATTHEW 6:3

"Restructure, define."
—UNKNOWN

"Fear stops you from speaking when it's your time to, or receiving what is rightfully yours."
—PASTOR JAY

"Don't be afraid to fail in this season, you will miss out on many opportunities that way."
—PASTOR JAY

"If you never ask, the answer is always NO."
—NORA ROBERTS

"The ONLY thing between you and your dream is FEAR."
—SHANNON SKINNER

"Miracles start to happen when you give as much energy to your dreams as you do to your fears."
—RICHARD WILKINS

"Fear is the only thing that can reduce your
energy and slow you down."
—UNKNOWN

"Drive more energy into your dreams and fear
will be left behind."
—UNKNOWN

"Nothing is Impossible… The word itself says
'I'm Possible'."
—AUDREY HEPBURN

"Do you give as much energy to your dreams as
you do to your fears? You will get what you want
when you stop making excuses for
why you don't have it."
—UNKNOWN

The Creator

I am a believer in a higher power, a spiritual being who is the mother of creation. Some may refer to God, others Yahweh, Jah, or the MOST HIGH depending on the religious attachment. I believe we, as children under one sun, should have a belief in something.

"Hear and recognize the voice of the Creator. When you hear from heaven it's time to go to the bank, and you don't need the assurance of man."
—PASTOR JAY

"Real religion is the transformation of anxiety into laughter."
—ALAN WATTS

"Faith is to believe what you do not see; the reward of faith is to see what you believe."
—ST. AUGUSTINE

"When you wake up in the morning put on your oil of anointing {PAM} all of the negativity hurt, depression, jealousy, and criticism won't stick."
—JOEL OSTEEN

"I DON'T NEED THEIR APPROVAL I HAVE THE
GOD'S APPROVAL."
—JOEL OSTEEN

"Cannot waste my time- keep moving forward
and God will put the right people in place for
you."
—JOEL OSTEEN

"Be responsible with the gift God has given
you."
—JOEL OSTEEN

"Those who believe in more than themselves
are agents of change on the earth."
—COOKI MANGO

"Have you heard a word about your neighbor;
let it die within you."
—JOEL OSTEEN

"This is your test. Don't believe everything you
hear. Be careful, be kind, and be respectful. Just
as wrong to be the EAR as it is the mouth."
—JOEL OSTEEN

"A brother is born for adversity; friends fail;
defend your family."
—JOEL OSTEEN

"Show honor even when it is not due. Just
because it is true does not mean you have to
repeat it."
—JOEL OSTEEN

"Mercy is the vaccine. Be a person of honor."
—JOEL OSTEEN

"See every opportunity as a gift. Count your blessings, and watch God multiply them exceedingly all the days of your life."
—JOEL OSTEEN

"The entrance of His word gives light."
—PASTOR JAY

"When you speak the Word, you command your situation to change."
—PASTOR JAY

"Our God has NO LIMITATIONS, NO FEAR."
—PASTOR JAY

"NOTHING changes the Word of God but the
Word of God changes everything."
—PASTOR JAY

"When we believe His word He will
bring it to pass."
—PASTOR JAY

"You are God's most prized possession, and
extremely valuable. Approved, equipped, and
empowered by God."
—JOEL OSTEEN

"Our value comes from the fact that
God has painted us. We are fearfully and
wonderfully made."
—JOEL OSTEEN

"New levels means new devils."
—UNKNOWN

"Prepare yourself for what God has called
you to do."
—JOEL OSTEEN

"Don't expect divinity from people. Have grace
for people to see them as they are."
—VOICE OF HOPE

"God loves you. He wants the best. Do not focus
on the disappointment."
—VOICE OF HOPE

"Do not relive the past. God lives in the
present."
-VOICE OF HOPE

"Trust in the LORD with all your heart and do
not lean on your own understanding."
-PROVERBS 3:5

"God gives you weakness to
make you stronger."
—UNKNOWN

"Always thank the Creator because victory is on the way."
—COOKI MANGO

"Praise is putting action behind your faith. When things do not look good in the natural remember we have a supernatural God."
—JOEL OSTEEN

"With God leading you into victory, you can always plan for increase. You can plan for restoration. You can plan for a comeback, and you can plan for victory because He is leading and guiding you in Jesus' name!"
—JOEL OSTEEN

"Indecision and delays are the parents of failure."
—GEORGE CANNING

"The moment that you prayed about something, God established a set time to bring it to pass. Know that your promise is scheduled and your answer is on the way."
—UNKNOWN

"When someone is criticizing you just overlook it, don't get offended, keep moving forward in the destiny God has for you."
—KERRY BLACKBURN

"The will of God will never take you where the grace of God will not protect you."
—BERNADETTE DEVLIN

"There is no such thing as WRONGFULNESS only RIGHTEOUSNESS. So people who are wrong need to be left behind."
—UNKNOWN

"The fruit of silence is prayer. The fruit of prayer is faith. The fruit of faith is love. The fruit of love is service. The fruit of service is peace."
—JD KEYS

"Do what God instructs you to do in the spirit."
—UNKNOWN

"You might lose friends, but you will never lose favor with God."
—UNKNOWN

"When you're going through difficulty and wonder where God is, remember, 'the teacher is always quiet during the test.'"
—CHRISTIE-ANN NOREGIA

"God has something BIG in store for you, but to get it you have to step on fear and march on by faith."
—PASTOR JAY

"Every thought, every action, every interaction you experience today are seeds that will bring a harvest tomorrow."
—UNKNOWN

"Seek Godly counsel in decision making. Take time for decisions to 'settle.' Pay attention to 'checks' in your spirit. Do not move forward without the peace of God."
—DR. GARY SMALLEY

Positive Thinking

A llowing myself the freedom to take time out and reflect on my life has opened a gateway for positive thinking. I can remember how I felt when I came to terms with being a single mother. My negative self-talk told me that "no man would ever want you.. you are worthless and damaged goods". I needed time out, time away, and time alone to put my life as a whole in perspective. My son was raised within a much more positive environment because I chose not to listen to my self-talk. These quotes will allow you to see life is all about balance:

"To find peace, we need to strike a balance
between remembering yesterday and
imagining tomorrow."
—UNKNOWN

"Every loss leads you to a gain, and every 'no'
takes you that much closer to a 'YES'."
—SUZE ORMAN

Mindfulness Practice
observing and grasping tendency as it arises
without acting on it

Success [səkˈsɛs]
noun
is simply a favorable outcome; the achievement
of something tried or planned

"Our greatest glory is not in never falling but in rising every time we fall."
—CONFUCIUS

"Be satisfied with success in even the smallest matter and think that even such a result is no trifle."
—MARCUS AURELIUS

"Most people are just about as happy as they make up their mind to be."
—ABRAHAM LINCOLN

"My time is too valuable. Shake it off and move forward."
—JOEL OSTEEN

"These ears are not garbage cans. I do not
want to hear that trash."
–JOEL OSTEEN

"An attitude of gratitude is one of the most
powerful instruments of change you can wield."
–DR. BRYAN SCHUETZ

"Our imagination is the only limit to what we can
hope to have in the future."
–CHARLES F. KETTERING

"If you do not see great riches in your future,
you will never see them in your bank account."
–UNKNOWN

"Success is not the key to happiness. Happiness is the key to success. If you love what you're doing you will be successful."
—THERESA CAPUTO

"The definition of insanity is doing the same thing over and over and expecting a different result."
—ALBERT EINSTEIN

"How you start your day is how you are going to live your day. And how you live your day is the way you live your life."
—LOUISE HAY

"Your mind is able to manifest things into reality."
—UNKNOWN

"Shut down negative thoughts about yourself."
—UNKNOWN

"Happiness is not a gift you wish for. It doesn't come from a person or a thing or circumstance. Happiness is a mindset. It is a choice that you are able to make for yourself."
—UNKNOWN

"If you have ever think you are too small to make a difference in the world, try sleeping with a mosquito."
—DALAI LAMA XIV

"What you permit, you provoke. What you allow, you encourage. What you condone, you own. Allow only thoughts, words, and actions that build greatness in your life. Before you know it you will reach new heights."
—KERRY BLACKBURN

Celebrate You

C elebrate good times... C'mon, let's celebrate, and have a good time! I used to believe that people who celebrated themselves were arrogant, pompous jerks who were stuck up. I got caught up in the social media zone of watching others succeed at their goals and life direction and ended up neglecting all of the great things I have done. In one of my sessions with my therapist, I was asked to create a list of positive things I had accomplished in my life from birth. When I completed my list I was then told "now think of the baby who died at birth." Every day that the sun rises we get a chance to start over, to make yesterday's wrongs right. I challenge you to create your own list of accomplishments from birth.

"It's okay to feel different, it just means
you are unique."
—MAX

"Not everyone will like you. Do not try to
convince anyone of your worth."
—JOEL OSTEEN

"Go where you are celebrated not tolerated."
—JOEL OSTEEN

"Everything great in the world comes from
neurotics. They alone have founded our
religions and composed our masterpieces."
—MARCEL PROUST

"See yourself as a masterpiece. You didn't accidentally become who you are."
—UNKNOWN

"You are one of a kind. Original, unique and there will never be another you."
—COOKI MANGO

"Live in terms of your strong points. Magnify them. Let your weaknesses shrivel up and die from lack of nourishment. Remember whatever traits you feed are the traits that will succeed."
—KERRY BLACKBURN

"You carry yourself the way you see yourself, and people see you the way you see yourself."
—PASTOR DOVER

"Carry yourself as royalty, and be proud of who God made you."
—PASTOR DOVER

"You are excellent in every way. Not your performance, your heart."
—UNKNOWN

"Stars do not struggle to shine. Rivers do not struggle to flow, and you will never struggle to excel in life because you deserve the best."
—CHERYL SOLOMONS

"Don't live for others views of you."
—UNKNOWN

"Sometimes we have to experience the bad so we can learn to appreciate the good."
—KERRY BLACKBURN

"The flower that blooms in adversity is the rarest and most beautiful of all."
—KERRY BLACKBURN

"Do what you need to do for you! In the end it is you left NOT people. Be proud that you are about yourself and not about people's needs. In the end your needs/ happiness is most important."
—KERRY BLACKBURN

"Open your eyes to the miracles happening around you every single minute."
—UNKNOWN

"You are imperfectly perfect. Just the
way you are."
—UNKNOWN

"KNOW YOUR WORTH AND VALUE."
—COOKI MANGO

"If you focus on planting seeds that you would
like to see grow then the harvest will take
care of itself."
—UNKNOWN

"No matter how many mistakes you make or how slow you progress, you are still way ahead of everyone who isn't trying."
—KERRY BLACKBURN

"You won't succeed at anything if you do not acknowledge your failure."
—UNKNOWN

Your Mind

T he mind is a terrible thing to waste, they say. I say your mind is the most powerful thing in the universe. The mind has the ability to manifest things into reality, both positive and negative. With your imagination, you can create the reality your heart desires. My personal acknowledgment of change has allowed my mind to accept my faults, and to believe in whom I am to become. As seasons change so will the information we receive. I hope the following quotes will allow your mind the freedom to receive positive vibes...

"What we think, we become."
—BUDDHA

"Start your day in a place of gratitude."
—UNKNOWN

"I WILL fulfill my own destiny."
—COOKI MANGO

"Everyone carries a bucket of water and a
bucket of gasoline. Will you add fuel to the fire?
Or put it out?"
—JOEL OSTEEN

"I have the ability to speak and
walk in authority."
—COOKI MANGO

"Your mind is a garden, your thoughts are
seeds. You can grow flowers or you can grow
weeds. Thoughts are things that shape your life
every single day. They are filled with energy but
luckily you get to choose the ones you want to
plant in the garden that is your mind.
Be sure to plant today what will bring the
harvest tomorrow. "
-UNKNOWN

"People get what they want in life when they reach the point at which they can see themselves having what they seek. When those thoughts become real in your mind you will develop the habits that are associated with having them. Visualize what you want in life and you will find it."

—KERRY BLACKBURN

"You are what you are and where you are because of what has gone into your mind. You can change what you are and where you are by changing what goes into your mind. Between our self-talk, the media, and the people around us we are constantly bombarded by manipulation. "

—KERRY BLACKBURN

"Life is 10% of what happens to me and 90% of how I react to it."
—CHARLES R. SWINDOLL

"The thoughts that begin your day will have a great effect on how the rest of your day works out. Feel the truth that every day is a gift from the Creator and open it like a child on Christmas day!"
—UNKNOWN

"Be careful of the thoughts you carry. The more you think about it the more you become it."
—UNKNOWN

"Impossible is not a fact. It's an opinion not a declaration. It's a dare. Impossible is potential. Impossible is NOTHING."
—MUHAMMAD ALI

"You come to love not by finding the perfect person, but by learning to see an imperfect person perfectly."
—SAM KEEN

"One of the hardest things in life is having words in your heart that you can't utter."
—JAMES EARL JONES

"Never ignore your inner voice, hunches, or sixth sense. They are calling you for a reason, and avoidance can be catastrophic."
—INGRID HOLM-GARIBAY

Determination

Determination to me is the act of finding your purpose and sticking to it. As an actor, it has been difficult to watch others advance in their careers, and not feel jealous. I needed to be reminded that no matter how many people do what I do, there is only one Christie " Cooki Mango No E" Maingot. At my lowest point, I was in the hospital days away from my 28th birthday, and I wanted to give up on life to cease the pain I was feeling. When I realized that my life can impact the lives of others, and most importantly my children's lives. No matter how much negative self-talk I was able to do to myself I could not think of or imagine another person that could love my children as I do. I hope one of these quotes can spark a flame within you to renew your determination in this life...

"How we see determines WHAT we see."
—UNKNOWN

"Suck it up. Accept that NOT everyone
will like you."
—DONNA BRAZILE

"View success as the ability to achieve a kind of
success that is its own reward- success based
on your own not society's values."
—UNKNOWN

"Walk with the dreamers, the believers, the
courageous, the cheerful, the planners, the
doers, the successful people with their heads
in the clouds and their feet on the ground. Let
their spirit light a fire within you to leave this
world better than when you found it."
—LAW OF ASSOCIATION

"When you are surrounded by people who expect more from you then you expect from yourself you produce more, you grow faster, you turn years into months. Look around and see whose business you want to model. People who are already playing that bigger game. That is the ultimate shortcut."
—KERRY BLACKBURN

"In order to succeed your desire for success MUST be greater than your fear of failure."
—BILL COSBY

"We have to do the prep work and trust the process."
—KERRY BLACKBURN

"The value of an idea lies in the use of it."
—THOMAS EDISON

"Four short words sum up what has lifted the most successful individuals above the crowd: A LITTLE BIT MORE. They did all that was expected of them and a little bit more."
—UNKNOWN

"Fall seven times and stand up eight."
—JAPANESE PROVERB

"Absorb what is useful; reject what is useless."
—BRUCE LEE

"Water is pretty hot at 211 degrees but it can't do many of the things that boiling water can do. It is the extra degree that will separate you from the crowd and bring you to a place of your dreams."
—RALPH WALDO EMERSON

"It's better to be organized than scrambled."
—MILLIE BUCKS

"Can't slow down progress."
—BOBBY COX

"In the confrontation between the stream and the rock; the stream always wins. Not through strength but by PERSEVERANCE. Rarely will life hand you a win without a test. Those tests will rarely be in short form answers. Learning to persevere through the challenges will build your strength, and make the wins more gratifying. Making you more grateful for the experiences you had to endure."
—H.JACKSON BROWN

"The difference between try and triumph is just a little 'umph'. If you don't go after what you want then you will never have it. The first step is always the hardest so stop thinking about it and just do it."
—MARVIN PHILLIPS

"Growth means many different things to all of us but the one thing it is for everyone is a process. Nothing becomes great all at once. Attempt each day to do more, be more, and love more."
—UNKNOWN

"Have the attitude that there are no limits on what you can accomplish because the only limits you have are the ones that you impose on yourself. Nothing is impossible for those that live without limits."
—KERRY BLACKBURN

"People that take the easy route do not get
lasting results."
—UNKNOWN

"Be proactive about taking responsibility for
your life."
—KERRY BLACKBURN

"The higher you climb up the ladder the more
your ass is exposed."
—CHRISTOPHER MAINGOT

"Just know when you truly want success you will never give up on it. No matter how bad the situation looks. Challenges are what make life interesting, and overcoming them is what makes life meaningful."
—UNKNOWN

"A dollar saved is a dollar gained."
—GEORGE HERBERT

"It is never too late to become who you wanted to be."
—GEORGE ELIOT

"Luck, timing, and persistence. Create opportunities for yourself."
—UNKNOWN

Final Thoughts

No matter how hard I have tried to be a people pleaser in my thirty-plus years of life, I have NEVER been a ME pleaser. I am a daughter, sister, niece, cousin, mother, teacher, sistah/friend, thespian, and I can always find new ways of helping other people but not myself.

Living according to how it makes me feel has been the most gratifying feeling. To know that I am in the pursuit of my happiness and aiming to succeed with my goals and aspirations brings me an uplifting feeling. I am finally experiencing feelings of accomplishment, although I have not yet attained my ultimate goals. I am crossing things off my list day by day. When I take time out to be with myself and my thoughts, now, I am pleased. This is, of course, opposed to months ago when I would hide in the bathroom or my closet to get away and be with my negative thoughts.

Negative thoughts became a part of who I was. "A worthless, ugly, piece of shit," is what I would call myself. It is how I perceived myself and where my mind was stuck. It took me punching a glass door, receiving thirteen stitches, banging my head against the drywall until there was an imprint of my forehead, and getting drunk and running away from my husband, to realize that I needed help.

No one else. It was me. The problem I had was within me, and I needed to make a decision.

Did I want to continue to live like this hating myself? Only a person who has no self-love could do such things to themselves. Did I want my two beautiful children to continually see their mother in a depressed state all the time? Was it fair for my husband to love me if I couldn't find the will to love myself?

For me, the answer was, "I need professional help! I need to go to a place where I am understood; where I will not be judged but listened to and set in the right direction."

For many years, I have self-medicated with cannabis. It helped for the moment to calm my thoughts and distract me from the main issue of my unwillingness to love myself. Temporary fixes are just that temporary. I found myself becoming dependent. I can't eat unless I smoke, I can't go to work unless I smoke, I can't go to sleep unless I smoke, and the list goes on. I was stuck in a rut. I was doing the same things over and over expecting a different result; the definition of insanity. I was going insane. So, I grew some balls, packed my bag, and left for the mental ward at the hospital. I did not want to be different from my friends, family, and co-workers. I wanted to be "normal," (yet I have always had an abnormal way of looking at life). I realize now that it is okay to be different, it just means I'm unique, and it is ok to seek help. I have been created to experience things in my way, to learn from my own experiences; to accept me for who I am.

Who I am?

'Who am I?' is what I needed to ask. What is it that I want out of life? Why do I want it? And what am I willing to do to get what I want? I realized that I couldn't look to my husband, parents, children, or brother, I had to look within.

"Life is like a box of chocolates, you never know what you are going to get. Much less if you're going to like any of the chocolates at all. Unless you try, taste, and try some more."
–COOKI MANGO

Love and Light,
Christie Maingot
@Cookimango_da_Goddess